J 921 EFRON ZA Pep
Peppas, Lynn.
Zac Efron /

RATH
JUN 1 3 2011

D0767909

Efron

By Lynn Peppas

Crabtree Publishing Company

www.crabtreebooks.com

Crabtree Publishing Company
www.crabtreebooks.com

Author: Lynn Peppas
Publishing plan research and development:
  Sean Charlebois, Reagan Miller
  Crabtree Publishing Company
Project coordinator: Kathy Middleton
Photo research: Crystal Sikkens
Editors: Molly Aloian, Kathy Middleton
Proofreader and Indexer: Wendy Scavuzzo
Designer: Ken Wright
Production coordinator and Prepress technician: Ken Wright

Photographs:
Associated Press: page 24
Corbis: © Phil Klein/Reuters: page 15
Getty Images: © Albert L. Ortega/Wire Image: page 14; © David Livingston/Stringer: page 17
Keystone Press: © Leo Rigah/Starlitepics: page 5; © BIG Pictures UK: page 6; © Rick Mackler/ zumapress: page 7; © Laura Dickinson/The Tribune: page 9; © Walt Disney Pictures/zumapress: pages 11, 22; © Mike Emory/Andy Athineos: page 12; © DS7/wenn.com; © The WB: page 16; © Nancy Kaszerman/zuma: page 19; © FOTOS International: pages 20, 23; © Offspring Entertainment: page 25; © CinemaNX: page 26; © Diyah Pera: page 27; © FAME Pictures: pages 1, 28
Retna Pictures: © Max Cisotti/Disney: page 21
San Luis Obispo County Visitors & Conference Bureau: page 8
Shutterstock: cover, pages 1, 4, 10, 18

Every effort has been made to trace copyright holders and to obtain their permission for use of copyright material. The authors and publishers would be pleased to rectify any error or omission in future editions. All the Internet addresses given in this book were correct at the time of going to press. The author and publishers regret any inconvenience caused if addresses have changed or sites have ceased to exist, but can accept no responsibility for any such changes.

Library and Archives Canada Cataloguing in Publication

Peppas, Lynn
  Zac Efron / Lynn Peppas.

(Superstars!)
Includes index.
Issued also in an electronic format.
ISBN 978-0-7787-7254-5 (bound).--ISBN 978-0-7787-7263-7 (pbk.)

  1. Efron, Zac--Juvenile literature. 2. Actors--United States--Biography--Juvenile literature. I. Title. II. Series: Superstars! (St. Catharines, Ont.)

PN2287.E395P46 2011   j791.4302'8092   C2010-905307-9

Library of Congress Cataloging-in-Publication Data

Peppas, Lynn.
  Zac Efron / by Lynn Peppas.
    p. cm. -- (Superstars!)
  Includes index.
  ISBN 978-0-7787-7263-7 (pbk. : alk. paper) --
  ISBN 978-0-7787-7254-5 (reinforced library binding : alk. paper) --
  ISBN 978-1-4271-9559-3 (electronic pdf : alk. paper)
  1. Efron, Zac--Juvenile literature. 2. Actors--United States--Biography--Juvenile literature. I. Title.
  PN2287.E395P47 2010
  791.4302'8092--dc22
  [B]
                                        2010032493

Crabtree Publishing Company

www.crabtreebooks.com   1-800-387-7650

Printed in the USA/102010/SP20100915

Copyright © 2011 CRABTREE PUBLISHING COMPANY. All rights reserved. No part of this publication may be reproduced, stored in a retrieval system or be transmitted in any form or by any means, electronic, mechanical, photocopying, recording, or otherwise, without the prior written permission of Crabtree Publishing Company. In Canada: We acknowledge the financial support of the Government of Canada through the Book Publishing Industry Development Program (BPIDP) for our publishing activities.

Published in Canada
Crabtree Publishing
616 Welland Ave.
St. Catharines, ON
L2M 5V6

Published in the United States
Crabtree Publishing
PMB 59051
350 Fifth Avenue, 59th Floor
New York, New York 10118

Published in the United Kingdom
Crabtree Publishing
Maritime House
Basin Road North, Hove
BN41 1WR

Published in Australia
Crabtree Publishing
386 Mt. Alexander Rd.
Ascot Vale (Melbourne)

CONTENTS

Words that are defined in the glossary are in
bold type the first time they appear in the text.

Zac Attack! ⭐

It takes just one look at American actor Zac Efron to recognize why fans and popular magazines call him a "tween heartthrob." A tween is a fun name for a young person who is eight years old or older, but not yet a teenager. Although tweens fall for his good looks, people of all ages cannot help but be starstruck by Zac's impressive acting, singing, and dancing talents.

He Said It

"**Musicals** are very different from other films. And as an actor, when you're preparing for one, you train an entirely different skill set altogether. And as an audience member, I know the feeling I have when I leave a musical is **unrivaled** by any other type of film. I love watching things blow up, but it doesn't really excite me—and I can't sing that on the way home. So, musicals are cool. They're unique, and I'm glad that we're doing more of them."
—Interview in *Los Angeles Daily News*, July 2007

He Said It

"Shower before you go to bed, and then sleep on your wet hair. Towel-dry it. In the morning, it's all messed up naturally. If you have that messed-up thing going when you wake up, it's more willing to stay that way. That's Zac's hair tip."
—Interview in *Time* magazine, November 2009

Looking Like a Superstar

With his all-American, boy-next-door look, Zac could be mistaken for someone in your very own classroom. Some fans like his tousled brown hair. Other fans like the sparkle in his baby blue eyes. Zac also has a **charismatic** smile that can light up a room (and any admirer's heart). Perhaps you're a fan of his high cheekbones, fine nose, and chiseled, masculine jawline. When you put these qualities together, it's easy to see how this young man went from being a normal high school student to a *High School Musical* movie star while he was still just a teen himself.

Just a Regular Guy?

No matter how many movies he's starred in, Zac remains **modest** and insists that he's just a "regular guy." He feels that the only difference between him and other actors his age is that he got the part of Troy Bolton in *High School Musical*.

He Said It

"I could show you 500 kids in L.A. who are my height, weight, hair color, and age. We're a dime a dozen. Why did I get the parts I did? Who knows? But the minute I start thinking it's because I was special, that's when I know I'm in trouble."
—Interview in *Toronto Star*, August 2007

Triple Threat

Zac might not be able to imagine how he got picked for the role of Troy Bolton, but it's pretty obvious that his talents as a performer played a big part. Zac is what is called a "triple threat." This means that he can act, sing, and dance— the perfect combination needed to perform in musicals. Not all actors have these three talents, but Zac certainly does!

High School Musical Mania

The first *High School Musical* movie was made for television by the Disney Channel in 2006. No one expected that it would become the huge hit that it did. At the time, it was the most successful movie that the Disney Channel had ever made. It was so popular that two *High School Musical* **sequels** followed—one on television in 2007 and one in theaters in 2008. Over 200 million people have watched *High School Musical* all around the world!

He Said It

"I was the worst kid on my 6th grade basketball team. I passed the ball to the wrong team and they scored at the buzzer in double over time to win the championship. Its one of those memories that STILL makes you squirm when you think about it!"
—On *Newsweek* online, July 2006

Fans from around the world love to pose with a wax figure of Zac Efron as Troy Bolton at Madame Tussauds wax museum in London.

A Normal Childhood

Zachary David Alexander Efron was born on October 18, 1987, in the county of San Luis Obispo, California. He was raised in the small city of Arroyo Grande, which has a population of less than 18,000 people.

Downtown Arroyo Grande

Zac's Childhood Home

San Luis Obispo is on the coast of California, halfway between Los Angeles and San Francisco. By California standards, Zac's hometown is kind of quaint. He calls it a "beach town." He has also described it as an **agricultural** area. His backyard looked out onto a farm.

From the time Zac was a young boy, his parents realized that he had musical talent. They helped Zac explore and study music, and even pushed him later to use his talent on stage. But Zac's parents had no way of knowing that their son would grow up to become the idol of millions—a singing, dancing, and acting superstar on stage and in the movies.

Meet the Efrons

Zac's parents are David and Starla Efron. They met at the nuclear power plant where they both worked. Starla was a receptionist and David worked as an engineer. Nobody in the family has a professional singing or acting background. Zac also has a younger brother named Dylan. Dylan is four years younger than Zac.

Zac said that as a young boy he used to sing around the house and in the car all the time. He said he sang so much that it used to "annoy" his parents. David and Starla thought it would be a good idea to enroll Zac in music lessons. Zac studied piano and singing. When he was eleven years old, his parents decided it was time for their son to try his talents out on the stage.

Growing up, Zac always enjoyed playing the piano.

Bitten by the Acting Bug

Although his parents were pretty sure he'd enjoy performing onstage, Zac himself wasn't

so sure. His mother tricked him into going on his first **audition** for a role in the musical *Gypsy*. He landed a role. The production, held at the Pacific Conservatory of the Performing Arts in Santa Maria, had a very successful 90-show run.

He Said It

"[My mom] asked me if I wanted to go to Toys 'R Us one day. I wanted one of those action figures or something, and little did I know it was actually a trick. She dropped me off for this audition for Gypsy. I ended up getting the part."
—On *The View*, April 2009

ARROYO GRANDE HIGH

Zac attended Arroyo Grande High School. *Glee* actor Harry Shum Jr. and Olympic gold medalist in discus Stephanie Brown Trafton also attended Arroyo Grande High.

"*I wasn't on the basketball team. I was pretty much a typical high school student…[I] was the coolest of the nerds.*"
—On *The View*, April 2009

Zac @ School

Zac was a straight A student in school. If he got anything less than an A he would be upset with himself. Zac's favorite subject at school was English. In middle school, he acted in musicals such as *Peter Pan, Little Shop of Horrors, Music Man*, and *Nifty Fifties*. His drama teacher recognized his acting ability. She suggested to Zac's parents that he find an agent and begin auditioning for acting roles. Zac and his mother began making the drive to Los Angeles for auditions. Zac said that for every role he did get on TV or in a movie, he'd probably have 30 or 40 auditions that he didn't get.

Zac poses as Troy Bolton, captain of the basketball team, in *High School Musical*.

Even though he played the part of Troy Bolton, who was captain of the basketball team in *High School Musical*, Zac said that as a teen going to Arroyo Grande High School, he was definitely more interested in doing drama than sports.

11

A Regular Childhood

In many ways, Zac's childhood was pretty typical. Like many North American teens, he liked skateboarding, playing video games, golfing, skiing, surfing, and snowboarding. He always maintains that he's just a "normal guy," doing normal-guy things—except, that is, for his love of theater and acting. In high school, Zac's friends nicknamed him "Hollywood."

A lot of magazines like to write about **controversial** things that teen stars do or say, or print photographs that are inappropriate. But Zac has kept a clean reputation, so far!

Zac still enjoys surfing the waves whenever he can. He was recently involved in a charity with pro-surfer Layne Beachley.

He Said It

"I don't have much to worry about...because my personal life isn't that interesting."
—Interview in *Time* magazine, August 2007

Kiss and Tell with Zac

Zac remembers his first kiss in a tree fort when he was in fifth grade. He was the only boy with a bunch of girls playing a game of "Truth or Dare," but it turned into a kissing game instead. At the time, Zac admitted he was "pretty stoked."

FIRST LOVE

In seventh grade, Zac had a **celebrity** crush on supermodel and actress Tyra Banks. He kept a poster of her in his room. He called her his "first love."

Supermodel Tyra Banks

The Big Screen

Zac began getting professional television acting jobs while still attending Arroyo Grande High School. He started getting small roles and guest appearances on TV shows as early as 2002. While most high school students are trying to decide what to do with their lives when they graduate, Zac was already working in his chosen line of work. Ready or not— Zac's career had already begun.

First TV Breaks

Zac's first appearance on TV was on the **sci-fi** show *Firefly*. The episode aired in November 2002. Other TV guest appearances followed. In October 2003, he appeared on the popular medical drama *ER* as a young patient named Bobby Neville who comes into the emergency room with a fatal gunshot wound. Then, in February 2004, he played a character named Luke Tomello in an episode of the series *The Guardian*.

Keeping It a Secret

Zac has never been one to brag about his acting career. He tried to keep it a secret from the other kids in his high school. It worked until the day Zac's math teacher asked the class if anyone watched *ER* last night. No one had, so the teacher pulled out a portable TV, hit play, and showed the class the taped episode of *ER* called "Dear Abby" with Zac's character Bobby Neville. Zac's teacher played it in each of his classes that day. His secret was out in the open from that day on.

Making Movies

In 2003, Zac started getting roles in TV movies, such as *Melinda's World* and *The Big Wide World of Carl Laemke*. In 2004, he played an **autistic** twin in the made-for-TV movie called *Miracle Run*. His performance earned him a nomination for a Young Artist Award for best performance in a TV movie. In 2005, Zac starred in *The Derby Stallion*. He played the lead role of Patrick McCardle, a horse-loving teen who is determined to win the Steeplechase Derby. It first aired on TV in July 2005.

Zac signs posters for *The Derby Stallion* for two young fans.

15

Summerland

Other guest appearances followed *ER*, but Zac's next big break came when he became a regular **cast member** on the dramatic TV series *Summerland* in June 2004. Zac was on 16 episodes of the show. *Summerland* is about the lives of three siblings, Bradin, Nikki, and Derrick Westerly. The three move in with their aunt who lives in California, after the tragic death of their parents.

Zac played Cameron Bale, a friend of Nikki Westerly's, in the TV series *Summerland*.

2006: Zac's Break-out Year

Zac was enjoying a successful career as an actor. He'd gone on to do more guest appearances on shows such as *CSI: Miami* and *The Suite Life of Zack & Cody*. He had six movie credits under his belt, too. But it was his role in *High School Musical* that catapulted Zac to superstardom.

The Magic Begins

High School Musical is a made-for-TV movie, which aired on January 20, 2006. The role of Troy Bolton was tailor-made for Zac's acting, singing, and dancing talents. The movie was instantly a huge hit becoming Disney Channel's most watched movie of 2006.

High School Musical is the story of East High School teen sweethearts Troy Bolton, the popular captain of the basketball team, and Gabriella Montez, a shy, smart girl. Song and dance break out everywhere as scheming students try to prevent the two from trying out for the school's musical. But in the end, talent—and love—win out. Troy and Gabriella sing and dance their way to the leading roles.

NO ZAC? NO WAY!

Actor Matthew Underwood of *Zoey 101* was offered the role of Troy Bolton first. He had to turn it down because it conflicted with his contract with the Nickelodeon television channel.

Zac (bottom right) poses with other **cast members** from *High School Musical*.

Facing the Music

Zac faced some **criticism** because his singing was blended, or **dubbed**, with singer, Drew Seeley's voice in the first *High School Musical* movie. Zac explained this was because the songs in the movie were written for a **tenor** singer. He is a **baritone** singer and the songs were out of his vocal range. But it's all Zac in *High School Musical 2* and *High School Musical 3: Senior Year*!

Zac loves Vanessa

In *High School Musical* and the sequels, Zac's love interest, Gabriella, is played by Vanessa Hudgens. Not only does she play Zac's leading lady on the screen, she has become his leading lady in real life, too.

Vanessa and Zac

Zac and Vanessa played their love interest roles so well, they were awarded a Teen Choice Award in 2006 for "TV–Choice Chemistry." But how much of it is an act? Zac and Vanessa are a real-life couple, and are often seen together at sports games, awards ceremonies, and even at the beach!

Music Video Hunk

What's a sure way to get the girls to watch your music video? Have Zac Efron play your love interest. In 2005, the pop singer Hope Partlow cast Zac as her love interest in her music video for the song "Sick Inside." The following year, he played the love interest in Vanessa Hudgens' music video for "Say OK." There probably wasn't too much acting needed in that one, though!

Zac Efron impresses an audience singing a song from the movie *Hairspray*.

He Said It

"We lip synch all the time. All the tracks [in High School Musical] are lip synched. That's not fully true. We're all singing [during filming]. We just don't record audio on the spot. The tracks are pre-recorded once beforehand. In regards to my voice, yes, it's my voice on the second High School Musical and also on Hairspray."
—Interview in *Toronto Star*, August 2007

Branching Out

High School Musical made Zac Efron a superstar! Suddenly, everyone around the world knew who he was. He has been on the cover of many music and fashion magazines, including *Rolling Stone*, *Teen Vogue*, and *GQ* (*Gentlemen's Quarterly*). *People* magazine listed him as one of the 100 Most Beautiful People in 2007. He hosted *Saturday Night Live* in 2009, and was interviewed on talk shows by Oprah Winfrey, Jay Leno, and Ellen DeGeneres. As Zac has grown up, his career has matured, too. What hasn't changed are his youthful looks, clean-cut reputation, and adorable modesty.

Hairspray

Zac's next big opportunity was the movie-turned Broadway musical-turned back into a movie, *Hairspray*. The quirky musical comedy about racial integration gave a much wider audience the chance to see Zac do his thing. As Link Larkin, the cool lead dancer on a 1960s teen dance show, Zac got to act alongside superstars Michelle Pfeiffer, Queen Latifah, and one of his heroes, John Travolta—who was playing someone's mom!

Zac (center left) and fellow cast members rock the set of the movie *Hairspray*.

20

High School Musical 2

High School Musical won many awards, including two Emmy awards for Outstanding Children's Program and Outstanding **Choreography**. Fans were begging for more. The following year, *High School Musical 2* was released as another TV movie. Sharpay and her crew try to break Troy and Gabriella up again—but this time they almost succeed. In the end, Troy and Gabriella share their first kiss.

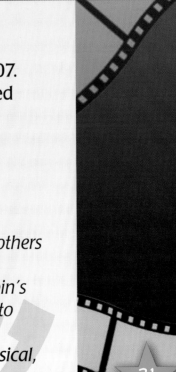

Zac greets fans at the premiere of *High School Musical 2*.

The first movie was a tough act to follow, but the sequel broke the record set by the original movie. Over 18 million people watched *High School Musical 2* the first time it was aired on television in 2007. It overtook the first movie as the highest-rated Disney Channel movie of all time.

She Said It

"We're like a family now. It's like living with brothers and sisters...Vanessa's like my shopping sister. Monique's the sister you go to advice for, Corbin's like the brother you always go to if [you need to talk], and Zac's the goofy one."
—Ashley Tisdale, Sharpay in *High School Musical*, in *People* magazine, 2007

High School Musical 3: Senior Year

The *HSM* ball just kept on rolling. *High School Musical 3: Senior Year* was released in October 2008, only this time it was in theaters, not on television. Our heroes, Troy and Gabriella, are finishing their final year at East High School. They are looking ahead to their futures at college and dreading being separated from one another. So what do they do? What else—they put on a show!

The third movie broke the record for largest opening weekend for a musical. It made $42 million in just three days!

Sing It, Zac!

Zac got to win back his reputation as a first-rate singer when he sang songs in *Hairspray*. "Ladies Choice" became the first single released from the movie soundtrack. There was no dubbing of voices. It was pure Zac vocals this time! The same was true for the soundtracks of *HSM2* and *HSM3*. Despite being a part of these bestselling soundtracks, Zac has no plans to do a recording of his own.

And the Award Goes To...

Zac's talent certainly hasn't gone unnoticed. He's been winning Teen Choice Awards since 2006, including Choice Breakout Star, Choice Movie Actor, Choice Male Hottie, and Choice Rockstar Moment. He has also earned MTV Movie awards for Best Male Performance (in *HSM3*) and Breakthrough Performance (in *Hairspray*).

NEXT GENERATION

A new *HSM* made-for-TV movie is planned, but Zac and Vanessa won't be in it since their characters have graduated. A new cast will be introduced in *High School Musical 4: East Meets West*.

23

What a doll...um, action figure!

Not many people can say that a doll was made to look just like them, but Zac can. In fact, there have been two dolls made in Zac's image. The toy company Mattel came out with a line of *High School Musical* character dolls that included one of Troy Bolton. Then another doll came out later based on Link Larkin, Zac's character in *Hairspray*. Which one does Zac prefer? Link Larkin. He was surprised how much it looked like him, much more than the Troy Bolton doll. "But," he told *Top of the Pops* magazine, "I still find it really strange that people want to collect them."

Zac poses with the Link Larkin doll. Zac's face also appears on a lot of *High School Musical* merchandise.

He Said It

"I've always seen my life going through college at one point and that's definitely a goal for me. I always got great grades going through school and I'm going to stay focused and do it eventually. But right now I've been a little bit busy."
—On *BBC Breakfast Morning Show*, August 2007

Moving On From High School

Although he was accepted into the University of Southern California in 2006, Zac decided to hold off on going to college so he could concentrate on acting. His career was hitting its stride, and since his *HSM* days were coming to an end, he thought it would be a good time to take risks and try roles that would challenge him.

WE MEET AGAIN

Actor Hunter Parrish appears with Zac in the movie *17 Again*. Parrish had also auditioned for the role of Troy Bolton and made it to the final five actors being considered.

He Said It

*"As I get older, I definitely get interested in certain kinds of films....Although I love musicals and continue to be in them, they are not the only **genre** I would love to do. I would love to try everything from horror to action to straight comedy—so much in this business that you can do and it's all in different levels."*
—Interview on PopEntertainment.com, August 2007

17 Again

In April 2009, Zac appeared in the comedy *17 Again*. In the story, a man is magically given the chance to see what his life would have been like if he had accepted a college scholarship. Zac plays the character after he transforms into his 17-year-old self. *17 Again* was a box office success and helped Zac prove he could act outside of musicals.

Zac Efron in *17 again*

25

Me and Orson Welles

Zac returned to the big screen to play yet another role of a 17-year-old in the film *Me and Orson Welles*. Zac plays Richard, an aspiring actor who is clearly out of his league in a Shakespearean play directed by legendary director Orson Welles. The movie was released in theaters in November 2009. Although not a box office hit like *17 Again*, movie reviewers liked it. Roger Ebert said it was "one of the best movies about the theater that [he's] ever seen."

He Said It

"[In Me and Orson Welles] there really wasn't a particular skill set that I could fall back on like singing, or dancing, or basketball...I wanted to come in, learn as much as I could, and also bring my A-game...I was incredibly nervous about the role and a bit scared at first..."
—Video interview for *Time* magazine's "10 Questions for Zac Efron," November 2009

Charlie St. Cloud

Released in theaters in July 2010, the film *Charlie St. Cloud* brought Zac in front of a wider audience. Zac starred in the drama about a young man grief-stricken over the loss of his brother. Playing someone who was feeling such raw emotion was a challenge he welcomed after working in comedies.

Taking Risks

Zac has said that he would like to focus more on expanding his acting abilities than on musicals for a while. With that in mind, he turned down the lead role in the remake of the incredibly popular musical movie *Footloose*. Instead, he has signed on to play a marine who searches for the girl who has been his goodluck charm in *The Lucky One*. He is also scheduled to play a college student hired by the CIA to become a secret agent in *Fire*, a comic book being brought to the big screen. Both movies are planned to be released in 2012.

LIFE
IS FOR
LIVING

Charlie St. Cloud (Zac) teaches his younger brother Sam (played by Charlie Tahan) how to pitch.

Picking Up Speed

Zac has studied, gone to auditions, and worked hard to make his dream of becoming an actor come true. John Waters, the creator of *Hairspray*, believes Zac is also "quite smart about it. He will be one of those teen idols who, with fair ease, will move on to good adult roles and have a good career."

Zac has also learned a lot about the business side of movie making. This humble but ambitious young man has just started his own production company called Ninjas Runnin' Wild Productions to try his hand at producing films by young, talented people who "aren't afraid to try new things." As he branches out to new projects, he is sure to gather even more fans of all different ages on his path to superstardom!

He Said It

"I'm a product of this generation and I know how smart we are. I know the material that we crave in movies today—we're not seeing a lot of it."
—In *Wonderland* magazine, September 2010

Timeline

1987: Zachary David Alexander Efron is born on October 18 in San Luis Obispo, California.

1998: Zac goes to his first audition and gets a role in the musical *Gypsy*.

2002: Lands his first television role on the show *Firefly*.

2003: Makes a guest appearance on the TV show *ER*.

2003: Plays roles in the TV movies *Melinda's World* and *The Big Wide World of Carl Laemke*.

2004: Guest stars on the TV show *The Guardian*.

2004: Appears in 16 episodes on the television series, *Summerland*.

2004: Gets his first starring role in the made-for-television movie called *Miracle Run*

2004: Plays Harry Fuller in the TV movie *Triple Play*.

2005: Stars in his first feature film, *The Derby Stallion*.

2005: Has a guest role in the TV show *CSI: Miami*.

2006: *High School Musical* is released on the Disney Channel, featuring Zac as Troy Bolton.

2006: Lands more guest appearances on the TV shows *Heist*, *The Suite Life of Zack & Cody*, *NCIS*, and *The Replacements*.

2007: *Hairspray* is released in theaters, and the *Hairspray* soundtrack is released in stores.

2007: *High School Musical 2* premieres on TV, and the soundtrack is released in the U.S.

2008: *High School Musical 3: Senior Year* is released in movie theaters.

2009: Costars in the film *17 Again*, which is released in April.

2009: Hosts *Saturday Night Live* in April and appears in an episode of the TV show *Entourage* in September.

2009: Costars in the film *Me and Orson Welles*, released in theaters on November 25.

2010: Stars in the romantic drama *Charlie St. Cloud*, which premiered on July 20.

2010: Forms his own production company called Ninjas Runnin' Wild Productions.

2010: Signs on to appear in the movies *The Lucky One* and *Fire*, both scheduled for release in 2012.

Glossary

agricultural Relating to farming

audition A job interview for an actor that includes acting out a particular character

autistic A mental disorder that hinders people from communicating with others or responding to the world around them

baritone The second-lowest male singing vocal range

cast member An actor who's a part of a performance

celebrity A person who is widely known

charismatic Describing a person who possesses great charm and the ability to attract people

choreograph To make up or create a series of dance steps to music

controversial Describing an event or subject that makes some people uncomfortable, and they disagree with it

criticism Statement of how good or bad something is

dubbed To add in someone else's voice to a performance or recording

genre A type or category of a movie or book

modest To not draw too much attention, or exaggerate, one's own good qualities

musical A play or movie that includes songs to help tell the story

sci-fi Short for science-fiction; a play or movie genre that includes fantasy situations

sequel A movie that carries on the same story line and characters from a previous movie

tenor The highest natural male singing vocal range

unrivaled Not like anything else

Find Out More

Books

Morreale, Marie. *Zac Efron Scrapbook*.
   New York: Scholastic Publishing, 2009.
Llanas, Sheila Griffin. *Zac Efron*. Mankato, MN:
   Capstone Press, 2010.
Edwards, Posy. *Zac Efron Yearbook 2010*. London,
   England: Orion, 2009.

Websites

Zac Efron
   www.imdb.com/name/nm1374980/
Zac's biography and list of his appearances
in movies, tv roles, and soundtracks

Zac Efron
   http://en.wikipedia.org/wiki/Zac_Efron

New Line Cinema
   www.hairspraymovie.com
Synopsis of the movie *Hairspray*

High School Musical:
   http://tv.disney.go.com/disneychannel/original
   movies/highschoolmusical/index.html
High School Musical 2:
   http://tv.disney.go.com/disneychannel/original
   movies/highschoolmusical2/
High School Musical 3: Senior Year
   http://adisney.go.com/disneyvideos/television/
   highschoolmusical/

Index

About the Author

Lynn Peppas is a writer of children's nonfiction books. She has always been a bookworm and grew up reading all the books she could. She feels fortunate to have been able to combine her love of reading and her love of kids into a career. Her work in children's publishing is a dream-job come true.

32